YOU'RE *gonna* EAT THAT!?

Adventures with
Food, Family, and Friends

JULIANA LIGHTLE

Copyright © 2019 by Juliana Lightle

Originally published 2020 by Dreamcatcher Books Angel Editions, Las Vegas, NM
Republished with permission 2022 by Tranquility Press, Georgetown, TX

ISBN: 978-1-950481-38-5

Photography by the author, Juliana Lightle, and her daughter, Ema Mowoe.
Cover and Book Design by Lucy Jimenez & Mitch Khoury, Cramer Marketing.

Cover and Book Design by
Lucy Jimenez & Mitch Khoury,
Cramer Marketing

Printed in the United States of America

Table *of* Contents

Introduction

03   You Are What You Eat

Family

04   My Mother Taught Me
06   Mom's Recipes and Family Stories
15   Black Raspberries
17   Butter Love
18   Grandmother Recipes and Stories
22   Father Learning to Cook
26   Swedish Baking
29   I Watched Movers Box Up a Life
30   African Stories and Recipes
36   Persian Recipes

Friends

39   Eating with Friends
42   Go-to-Protein
49   Vegetarian
55   Lazy Day and Dinner
57   Italian
59   Costa Rica
66   Other

70   **Final Thoughts on Food and Life**

71   **Acknowledgments**

72   **Index of Recipes**

INTRODUCTION

One hot, early August afternoon results of an inane Facebook quiz gave birth to this book. Instead of "If you were a famous artist, which one would you be," this one suggested that a certain quote could define your personality, your essence. A friend had posted her results so, a bit curious, I thought, "Why not?" I watched the little rainbow circle whirl, read the result, then laughed loudly. "You're gonna eat that!?" stared back at me.

This exact question actually pops into my mind rather often when I see what people eat at restaurants, dinners, potlucks, and what they purchase at the grocery. How did Facebook know? I never say this aloud. Admittedly, I created Facebook posts, emails, and even blog posts quoting one of Dad's mantras, "You are what you eat!"

My secret was out there for all to see. Instead of snarky comments, followers and friends commented, "Write a cookbook." My daughter went even further, insisting, "Mom, you have to do this."

My recipes come from years of interaction and relationships with people from all over the world, from relatives, especially my mother, from husbands, exchange students, my extended family, requests from friends who come regularly to my house for dinner, from my efforts to create successful meals for vegetarian friends, and from travels to Asia, Africa, Latin American.

Here you will find not only recipes but also memories, stories, and poems, tributes to people, places, and food I have experienced and loved. With this book, I invite you to step into my world of food, family, friends, and adventure.

Enjoy!

"You are what you eat!"

Dad's mantra. Health food obsessed before it became fashionable, he took us to one of the first health food stores in the country, 90 miles away in downtown Kansas City. Even so, he never cooked before Mom died.

His adored mother died from diabetes at 65; she had stashed her sweet killers in closets, drawers, under the bed, hidden.

He married Mom late at 38. She grew a vegetable garden 60 by 100 feet or so. Spring vegetables—lettuce, radishes. Summer vegetables—tomatoes, broccoli, peas, cabbage, beets, green beans, cucumbers. Turnips and parsnips in the fall. Vegetables surrounded with zinnias—red, orange, hot pink, yellow. Dad kept a Percheron to plow the garden in spring. Mom's orders. She said a tractor smashed the soil too much.

Dad grew sweet corn encircled by hot wire to keep the raccoons out. Mom froze whole ears. Corn on the cob, a winter treat. I can taste it now: barely cooked in salted, boiling water, rolled in melted butter, crunching between my teeth, butter running down my chin.

All summer we helped ourselves to crocks full of pickled beets with hard boiled eggs, golden yolks encircled in deep red-purple. I ate them just to see the color contrast, their beauty.

Mom froze vegetables. "More like fresh," she said. Except tomatoes; she canned those. After she died, I took the quart mason jars left over, rationed them, made my own spaghetti sauce, a dish Mom never made. No canned brand, even when I doctored them, could duplicate Mom's. She never left that recipe.

MY MOTHER TAUGHT ME

Black and white perspectives,
guidelines to live a productive
proper life, to be a good woman
doing good deeds for good people.

I rarely contemplate her rules for life,
realize I follow many of them-
passed on to my daughter.
Mother baked and cooked and cleaned,
loved Shetland ponies and horses.

How to make a cake:
    -grease and flour the cake pan
    -cut out circles of waxed paper to put on top the
     greased and floured surface (you do not want the
     cake to stick)
    -sift the flour
    -soften the butter
    -mix the ingredients in exactly this order

What to wear:
    -clean underwear in case of a car wreck
    -coordinated clothes
    -polished shoes
    -purse and shoes to match
    -no white anything before May 1 or after September 1,
     excluding underwear of course

How you present yourself to the world:
    -well groomed
    -clean fingernails
    -self assured
    -nice, but not too nice
    -polite
    -brushed teeth
    -lotioned body
    -clean, shiny hair

How to wash your clothes:
    -separate whites and colors
      (you want your whites to stay snowy)

How you ride your pony:
    -keep your heels down
    -don't lean back too far
    -hold the reins between loose and tight
    -kick the sides once to trot and click your tongue
    -kick twice to canter and click your tongue a bit more
    -pull the reins back to stop

How you clean your house:
    -vacuum first, dust second
    -if you do not do it right the first time, you will have to do it over

This is how you breathe to sing.
This is how you practice well.

Mother could barely sew and could play the piano only a little by ear,
by changing from sharps to flats. I had to learn to play the piano and sew;
it was mandatory. Now I sew only when a button is off or
hemming is needed, or better, cheaper curtains.

Mother could really bake, especially pie.
Her crusts were tasty works of art.
At potlucks, people would get her pie first to make sure they got some.
At potlucks now, people get my pie first to make sure they get some.
At potlucks now, people get my daughter's pie first to make sure they get some.

Mother loved her ponies.
I love my horses: once I owned forty thoroughbreds and quarter horses.
Now I have two. I ride, my daughter rides, my grandson rides.
I wonder: will his children bake and ride?

BACK TO CHILDHOOD

When I think back to childhood, I recall eating a sort of pet calf but never our pet pigs. Dad raised registered Hampshires. When a sow rejected a runt, Dad gave it to my sister or me. Then it lived in the kitchen in a box and drank from a bottle until it became strong enough to go back to the hog house. We gave them names. Even when grown, moms on their own and out free in the woods behind the house, they came running when called. I named my favorite Betsy.

Mom occasionally baked pork chops bought at the grocery. Here is Mom's handwritten recipe.

All these recipes from mom and grandmother remain exactly as they wrote them.

a family Favorite recipe

Mom's Pork Chops

Ingredients

6 pork chops
1 cup rice
1 can cream of mushroom soup
½ cup milk
salt to taste

Directions

Brown 6 pork chops in skillet. Cook 1 cup rice, salt to taste. Mix rice with one can cream-of-mushroom soup & ½ cup milk. Spread rice mixture in baking dish or sheet pan & top with pork chops. Bake in oven until chops are tender.

Mom's Salmon Loaf

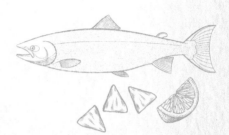

Ingredients

1 can red salmon
3 T lemon juice
4 T melted butter
1 t salt
dash of pepper
3 eggs slightly beaten

1 medium-sized pkg of
potato chips
- or -
3 cups corn flakes or
Wheaties

Directions

Crush chips a little if using chips. Break salmon into large flakes. Combine with other ingredients. Pack into a buttered baking dish. Bake 20 minutes in a medium hot oven. Variations: Add one can cream of celery soup or whole kernel corn, add one cup grated cheese, or use crackers instead of chips or cereal.

Mom never used the variations and must have used Wheaties or crackers because we never ate cornflakes and rarely ate chips.

As I began writing this book, favorite dishes Mom cooked crept into my consciousness, dishes like salmon cakes and the angel food cake we all requested for birthdays. After repeated attempts searching for her recipes for both, I gave up, disappointed. I especially wanted to make the salmon cakes. I loved Mom's salmon cakes, have never eaten others quite so yummy, and have never been able to duplicate them.

As I write this my taste buds come alive, remembering those salmon cakes which she always served with creamed peas, not canned peas—we never ate canned peas, but ones we had grown in the garden, spent hours shelling, then froze. One year we put up over 100 pints. I was just a kid with thumbs aching from so much shelling; I went on a strike against eating peas, thinking never again will I have to do this. I am going to hate peas forever. I don't.

The closest recipe I could find to salmon cakes is this recipe for a salmon loaf that she had typed up for me.

THE RECIPE BOX

This recipe box contains recipes I began collecting and organizing decades ago when newly married at 20. Many of them Mom typed on cards, sometimes adding handwritten comments. Her tea cookies, pumpkin bread, and pumpkin pie remain annually baked for Thanksgiving-Christmas. Others are a rediscovery, recipes once often used but forgotten until recently. This past weekend I invited my daughter and grandson to dinner to cook this recipe, one of those once-upon-a-time, favorites, forgotten until recently when I found it in the box. In spite of the name, these are really meatballs.

I mixed this with my hands, shaped into round balls about 1½ - 2 inches in diameter, and browned in oil in a non-stick, deep skillet. Mom used the tomatoes she canned herself. Now, I use either commercial crushed or diced tomatoes and brown sugar.

As this simmered, the smells of the farmhouse where I grew up, the sound of Mom always singing as she cooked, the view across the garden, they all came back — the smell of home and family and the love we shared, a love of healthy food, our close family, beauty, home.

Mom always served this with mashed potatoes. To be true to her tradition, I serve them with mashed potatoes even though pasta seems to make more sense.

It occurs to me that after browning the meatballs, a slow cooker would work perfectly to complete the process. I could double or triple the recipe and feed a mini crowd and serve directly from the slow cooker.

My fourteen-year -old grandson helped, fascinated by the old metal box with the lost lid, that old box full of family recipes. He announced that he wants his own recipe box and plans to copy the recipes, determined to carry on family traditions.

---

a family *Favorite* recipe

Mom's Hamburger with Tomatoes

Ingredients

1 ½ lbs. ground beef
¾ cup oatmeal
¼ tsp. pepper

1 egg
¼ cup cream
2 tbs. sugar

Directions

Mix well and shape into patties, brown on both sides; cover with tomato juice. Slice one large onion over the top of the patties, add a sprinkle of salt, and 2 T sugar. If tomatoes are quite sour, add enough sugar to make sweet. Cook slowly, turn meat occasionally.

A recipe never forgotten, often used out of the usual season, is Mom's Pumpkin Bread. After trying numerous other recipes, I always revert back to this one. During the holiday season, I bake several batches for presents. Mom hand wrote this recipe exactly as below.

I do not mix this in the order below. I mix the oil, sugar, and eggs together first, then add the dry ingredients. I also cut the sugar back to 2 cups, but then I cut out about ⅔ of the sugar in everything I bake.

I bake the Pumpkin Bread in three 13-ounce coffee cans. This allows me to make three versions:
- one plain with no nuts or raisins, using ⅓ of the batter
- one where I add 1 cup chopped walnuts to the remaining batter and place ½ of that in the second can
- one where I add ½ cup golden raisins to the remaining batter and place it into the last can.

The small cans make perfect-sized loaves for gifts. Those who like plain get the first loaf, those who want just nuts receive the second loaf, and those who want it all receive the loaf with both nuts and raisins.

a family Favorite recipe

Mom's Pumpkin Bread

Ingredients

3 cups flour
1 tsp cinnamon
1 tsp nutmeg
1 tsp salt
1 tsp soda
1 tsp baking powder
½ tsp cloves

½ tsp allspice
1 cup cooking oil
3 cups sugar
3 eggs well beaten
1 tsp vanilla
1 can pumpkin *(small)*
⅔ cup nuts *(walnuts or pecans)*

Directions

Sift together flour, cinnamon, nutmeg, salt, soda, baking powder, cloves, allspice. Add cooking oil, sugar, eggs well beaten, vanilla, pumpkin. Mix well, add nuts. Grease 3 coffee cans and flour good. Fill each can half full. Bake 350 oven 1 hour or more, test with a tester or broom straw.

FALL FAVORITES

Mom's Bran Muffins

Ingredients

1 cup All-Bran
(or another bran cereal)
¾ cup milk
1 egg

¼ cup soft shortening
1 cup sifted flour
2 ½ t baking powder
½ t salt
¼ cup brown sugar

Directions

Combine bran and milk, let stand until most of the moisture is taken up. Add egg and shortening; beat well. Add brown sugar. Sift together flour, B.P., and salt. Add this to the mixture, stirring only until combined. Fill greased muffin pans ⅔ full. Bake in 400 degree oven 30 min.

Sweet Sautéed Apples

Core and slice several apples. Do not remove skin. Melt enough butter in a skillet to cover the bottom about ⅛ inch thick. Place sliced apples in the melted butter one layer only. Sauté until translucent. Sprinkle white sugar over the apples and allow to melt, then stir the apples. If properly sautéed, a thin glaze will form over the apples. Serve warm.

Although we raised hundreds of hogs, we ate little pork. Dad disliked ham, thought little of bacon, but liked sausage occasionally. We bought sausage at the store. One of my favorite childhood suppers included sausage, scrambled eggs, bran muffins, and sautéed apples. I am guessing Mom may have acquired the muffin recipe she used from an All-Bran box. Perhaps not. Her recipe does not match the current recipe on the box.

The reverse side of Mom's recipe card contains all sorts of variations she never used. While we may have buttered our own muffins, my personal favorite was to put the sautéed apples on top and eat with a fork. There is no recipe for this so above is a description of how to sauté apples. We always used Jonathan apples, purchased from a nearby orchard. Where I live now, I never see this kind of apples. You must use a type of apple that does not disintegrate when cooked, one that stays firm and holds its shape.

MOM'S PIES

Mom's pies made her famous at our country church potlucks. When people arrived, they looked for her pies first, hid a piece so they would get one. Her handwritten recipe for pie crust resides in my pantry in that worn 3 by 5 by 2 metal box.

When writing this, I realized I have never owned a pastry blender. I always use a fork. I also realized I have no idea whether Crisco still exists, but like Mom, I still roll the crust out between two sheets of waxed paper and wet down the surface to keep the paper from sliding, just like Mom did. I use her old roller; I think of her, barely five feet tall, a tiny powerhouse of a woman, pretty with big blue-grey eyes, short, wavy, brown hair, always singing or humming to herself while she worked. In old photos from her younger years, her then blonde self is always smiling. Mom was not a crier.

My grandson will only eat the pumpkin pie from her recipe, none other. His cousin asks me, "Where's my pumpkin pie" every time she sees me--summer, winter, any time. She loves mom's pumpkin pie. She is 15. This last Thanksgiving, my grandson insisted on learning to make it himself. We made two of them.

I use oil instead of Crisco.

a family
Favorite
recipe

Mom's Pie Crust

Ingredients

2 cups flour
1 tsp salt
2/3 cups Crisco
1/3 cup ice cold water

Directions

Mix flour and salt together. I use pastry blender for this. Add shortening, cut in with the blender until about the size of small peas. Add water a little here and there and mix with a fork

Mom's Pumpkin Pie

Ingredients

1 ½ c cooked or canned pumpkin
1 ½ c milk or milk and cream or evaporated milk
3 eggs
¾ c brown or white sugar
½ t.salt
1 t cinnamon
1 t nutmeg
½ t ginger (or use ½ t nutmeg and 1 t ginger for more spicy flavor)

Directions

Place your hand on blender cover before starting motor. Blend just a few seconds, until smooth, and pour into pastry lined shell. Bake at 450 for ten minutes, then bake at 350 for 30 minutes longer, or until firm in the center. A piece of outer peel of orange can be blender-grated into the pie. Add ½ cup of milk at the beginning and blend fine before adding other ingredients.

The actual recipe Mom gave me is on a typed card she enclosed in plastic. Inside, she stuck this personal note, handwritten on a separate, tiny sheet of paper.

"Juliana—if you use half evaporated milk it gives wonderful flavor and I like white sugar best"

I always use a can of pumpkin and only evaporated milk. I do not recall Mom ever putting orange peel in the pie. I never do. This is the only pie I make for Thanksgiving and sometimes for Christmas. It is a family tradition I feel close to and do not want to break. It reminds me of my happy childhood and my mom's unconditional love.

BLACK RASPBERRIES

Mom filled the white bowl with
black raspberries.
I poured Bossie's white cream over them,
watched it form a pattern,
flowing around the raspberries —
a design in deep purple and white.
I thought it almost too beautiful to eat.
I was seven.

Now I rarely find black raspberries. Red ones won't do. They lack the intensity, the beauty. Every year we went to Hunt's orchard north of Amazonia, Missouri, to buy black raspberries, took them home, sorted them to discard the imperfect ones, which we threw way behind the garden next to the timber—huge trees, oak and hickory.

Eventually, these transformed into thriving black raspberry bushes. We had our own black raspberry patch, created from the discarded, the imperfect.

Mom fed us fresh raspberries for a few days. The rest she used to create her famous pies, stocked a freezer full. Baked, they transformed a winter kitchen into the warmth and sweetness of my mother's family devotion.

On a humid summer day on a trip back to Missouri with my daughter and grandson, we found Hunt's Orchard. Shocked to find it still in business, we stopped. I told the proprietor that I used to come there as a child. We asked about black raspberries. "Too late, " he said. "The season's over."

I bake pies, many kinds of pies. I have never made a black raspberry pie.

One Egg Cake and Ice Cream

Although Mom baked special desserts for holidays, birthdays, and other special occasions, her go-to everyday dessert was One Egg Cake. It was the first recipe she taught me to make, a family recipe, a treat reserved for just us, our little close-knit family, a treat only available after we ate all our meat and vegetables.

It's quick, easy, and served warm immediately out of the oven brings back a rush of memories: the view out the kitchen windows of garden, greenery in summer, red and orange leaves in autumn, winter's lush snowfall and the many species of birds around Mom's bird feeder, family love and laughter year-round. Usually, she served it warm with ice cream, the pinnacle of treats.

Because we lived 30 miles from a sizable town, St. Joseph, getting ice cream home, unmelted, became a daunting task requiring dry ice. If you want to take frozen food cross country, use dry ice. It is solid carbon dioxide. Fog machines use it to make fog. Do not touch it; it will burn you! Once we arrived home with the ice cream packed in the ice and unloaded the ice cream, we took the ice outside and watched the "fog" form and blow away. It never ceased to fascinate.

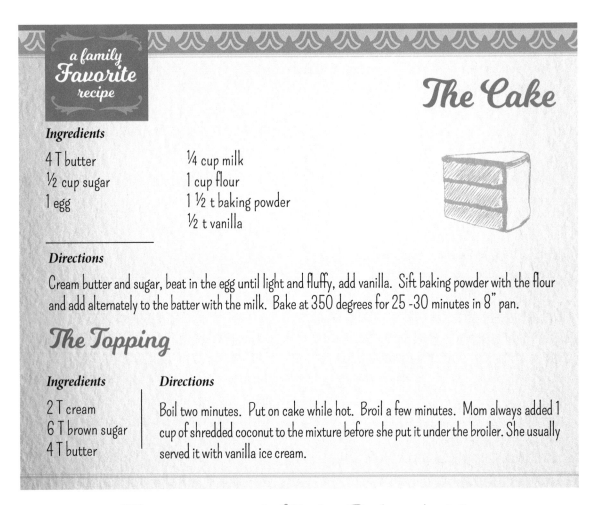

a family
Favorite
recipe

The Cake

Ingredients

4 T butter
½ cup sugar
1 egg

¼ cup milk
1 cup flour
1 ½ t baking powder
½ t vanilla

Directions

Cream butter and sugar, beat in the egg until light and fluffy, add vanilla. Sift baking powder with the flour and add alternately to the batter with the milk. Bake at 350 degrees for 25 -30 minutes in 8" pan.

The Topping

Ingredients

2 T cream
6 T brown sugar
4 T butter

Directions

Boil two minutes. Put on cake while hot. Broil a few minutes. Mom always added 1 cup of shredded coconut to the mixture before she put it under the broiler. She usually served it with vanilla ice cream.

This recipe is signed, "Mother, Barbara Lightle".

MY GRANDMOTHER

Grandma, Mom's mom, never smiled. People associate grandmothers with treats, spoiling, love. I'm certain she loved me; I do not recall her ever cooking me anything. When Mom went to the hospital to have my sister, the family story relates that Grandmother fed me so many bread, butter, and sugar sandwiches that I became fat. I was two. I remember a mint patch in her backyard. She'd gather the mint, boil water, make mint tea with sugar and cream added. I liked it. Grandma loved butter. When Aunt Julia went out of town, I remember seeing Grandma actually eat butter.

BUTTER LOVE

Is it inherited?

*Six year old me watched Grandmother
look around, take silver knife, cut into pale
yellow rectangular prism, plop a chunk into
her mouth, close her eyes,
smile.*

*In Aunt Julia's presence, this never occurred.
Was it our shared secret,
Grandmother and me?*

*Yesterday, I told the cafeteria lady,
"Please bring me biscuits, extra butter."
Less courageous than Grandmother,
I use blue corn pancakes, homemade bread, pasta.
excuses to eat butter, lots of golden, melted
butter.*

*Who eats butter on conchiglie?
I do, scooping out a tablespoon
from the butter bowl, watch it melt
in hot, drained Italian pasta from a
six-hundred-year-old monastery,
sprinkle on some sea salt, plop
a spoonful in my mouth, close my eyes,
smile.*

Mother and Grandmother

Old fashioned Dumplings

1 cup sweet milk ½ cream (½ + ½)

1 level ts B.P.

1 level ts salt

Flour enough to make soft dough to cut
into squares . make dough like soft
biscuit dough + pat out to thickness
of about ¼ in — cut in squares . Have
a bowl of flour to drop each square in
before adding to broth. May place several
in flr at once. Have broth to a rolling
boil — turn flame low drop in dumplings
+ try to space them Cook 10 min with
lid off and 10 min with lid on.

Grand mother Duke.

Noodles .

1 Egg

3 tb or ¼ cup Cream

1 Pinch salt

1 ts level B.P.

Work in as much flr as possible before
rolling out dough. Roll very thin and
place on paper to dry before cutting.
Cut finely about like this ▭
Grand mother Duke.

Grandma and Aunt Julia lived together. Aunt Julia ruled their household. Once Mom bought Grandma a pretty, floral summer dress. Aunt Julia made Mom return it, said it was too bright. She made Grandma wear old-lady lavender.

Aunt Julia made the best strawberry preserves. I used her handwritten recipe for years, shared it with friends. Sadly, I can no longer find the recipe. I am still searching.

The only other dish I recall Aunt Julia cooking is stewed liver. Yes, stewed liver—beef liver in a thick sort of broth with sage. The recipe, you ask? None exists. And, yes, I remember this because I liked it.

On Saturdays when Mom, my sister, and I drove the 30 miles to St. Joseph, Missouri, where I took music lessons, sometimes we stopped for lunch at their house there. Aunt Julia made sandwiches out of white bread, pickle-pimento loaf, fresh tomatoes, and Miracle Whip. We never ate white bread at home; Mom and Dad said it was not good for you. We rarely ate processed meat either. Same reason I suppose. I loved those sandwiches on a hot summer day, soft, squishy bread, cold lunchmeat contrasting with the rich juice of ripe, red tomatoes, tangy Miracle Whip. Occasionally in summer, I violate the eat healthy rule, go to the store, hunt down this lunchmeat, purchase just enough for a couple of sandwiches, drive home, indulge with a glass of icy milk.

Searching family recipes, I found a handwritten recipe in Grandma's hand, a recipe for noodles. I read it, astonished because I do not remember it or ever making homemade noodles. Occasionally Mom made chicken with noodles. Did she use this recipe?

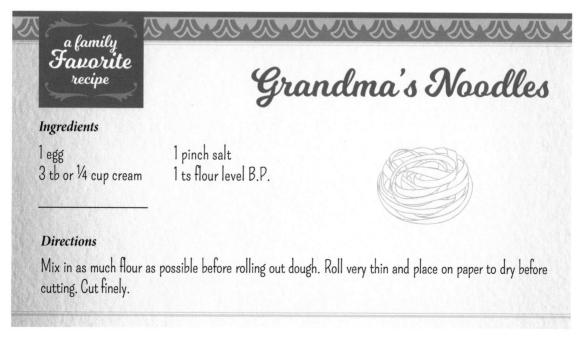

a family
Favorite
recipe

Grandma's Noodles

Ingredients

1 egg
3 tb or ¼ cup cream

1 pinch salt
1 ts flour level B.P.

Directions

Mix in as much flour as possible before rolling out dough. Roll very thin and place on paper to dry before cutting. Cut finely.

Strawberry Shortcake

1 level teacup sugar
½ cup melted butter
2 well beaten eggs
1 large pinch salt
2 Rounding teaspoons Baking Powder
1 cup sweet milk
enough flour to make a
Rather stiff dough.
Bake in two layers.
Butter while Real warm
and put on well crushed
Real sweetened Berries

I Melt Butter Put in my sugar
and stir well then a little
of the milk until the sugar
and Butter is wet enough
until it wont lump my
eggs then Beat hard and
add the Rest of ingrediants

Mother Duke

In a later search through the metal recipe box, I found another recipe of Grandma's, one for strawberry shortcake. Even though Mom loved it, she rarely made it because Dad did not like real strawberry shortcake. Occasionally, we grew just enough strawberries to have some fresh. Dad wanted them chopped up with a little sugar to eat over warm One Egg Cake without the topping. Grandma wrote this recipe in pencil. I had to put on my glasses and turn on bright light to read it because time had faded it so much.

"I had to put on my glasses and turn on bright light to read it because time had faded it so much."

Strawberry Shortcake

Ingredients

1 level teacup sugar
2/3 cup melted butter
2 well beaten eggs
1 large pinch salt
2 rounding teaspoons baking powder
1 cup sweet milk
enough flour to make a rather stiff dough

Directions

Bake in two layers. Butter while real warm and put on well crushed Real sweetened Berries. Do Not Flavor with anything

I Melt Butter, Put in sugar and stir well then a little of the Milk until the sugar and Butter is wet enough until it wont Lump my eggs. Then Beat hard and add the Rest of the ingredients

FATHER LEARNING TO COOK

Dad never cooked. He was too busy farming. When I was 11 or 12, he spent a lot of time in Colorado for a couple of years and hired someone else to plant and harvest the crops. We stayed home, Mom managed things, kept the garden going, sent my sister and me off to school. After school was out, we went to Colorado for the summer. Occasionally, Dad informed us of something he had discovered while away, usually some sort of food or interesting historical information. While rummaging through that recipe box, I found this recipe from Dad, typed on a 3 by 5 card.

```
WINE SAUCE
2/3 measure of sugar
stir in water until full
next day add 1/4 measure of Virginia Dare Wine
                          -Daddy
```

Fantastic on ice cream!

After Mom died, Dad had to learn to cook some since he lived alone 18 miles from the nearest town of any size. Mostly, he lived on canned salmon and canned spinach. However, the one thing he did learn to cook was pumpkin pie without the crust. No crust for a reason because a few years before he had learned he was very gluten intolerant. He did not use Mom's recipe. He probably had no idea where to find it. He used the one on the can of pumpkin. When I went to visit, he made it. Given his decades-long lack of cooking experience, its

perfection astonished me. I could hardly believe it. He simply followed the recipe on the can and, after lightly greasing a pie pan, poured the filling in it and baked it exactly as if the crust were there.

The one thing he did ask me to make was Mom's celery and potato soup for which she never used a recipe. This recipe is solely guessing from recollection. I made a large portion of it without adding the milk and told him he could just add milk as he wanted. Here are the basic directions.

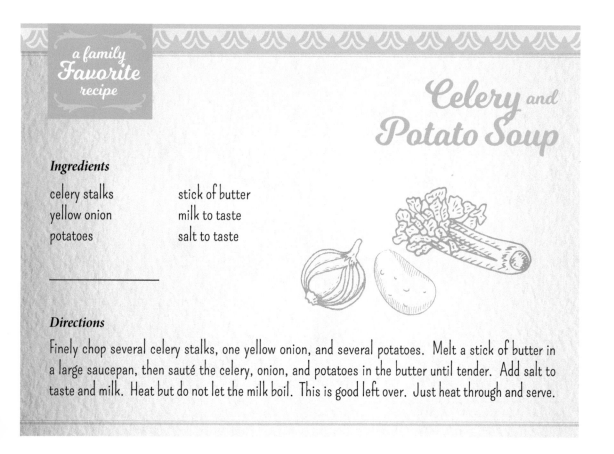

a family *Favorite* recipe

Celery and Potato Soup

Ingredients

celery stalks
yellow onion
potatoes

stick of butter
milk to taste
salt to taste

Directions

Finely chop several celery stalks, one yellow onion, and several potatoes. Melt a stick of butter in a large saucepan, then sauté the celery, onion, and potatoes in the butter until tender. Add salt to taste and milk. Heat but do not let the milk boil. This is good left over. Just heat through and serve.

It would probably be good with crumbled up bacon added, but we rarely ate bacon.

Few things compare to cooking while watching storm clouds race outside the great room windows especially when I lived on the edge of a canyon in the Panhandle of Texas where storms perform dramatic feats of wonder. Now I live in the San Gabriel Valley of California where I see bougainvillea and roses blooming in my lawn and mountains looming in the distance.

SWEDISH BAKING

My first mother-in-law, Gretchen Karlsson, created excellent meals and led me to new dishes and food combinations previously not experienced. She tended toward European dishes, including spices from her husband's Swedish traditions. I remember the bread in particular—made from rye flour flavored with cardamon. I associated cardamon with food from India and wondered how it became the mandatory spice of traditional Swedish baking.

Cardamon remains popular throughout Scandinavia. It dates back to the Viking era when those audacious adventurers discovered it in what is now Turkey. Today the European Union imports more than 1200 tons of cardamon per year. The main market is Sweden.

Even though I eat little bread, the following recipe has become part of my Christmas traditions, made every year for decades. I give away some and keep a little for myself. And yes, it contains rye flour and cardamon. It is my adaptation of a supposedly Finnish recipe baked traditionally at Easter. It makes three loaves.

Rye Bread *with* Cardamon

Ingredients

2 packages yeast
½ cup lukewarm water
1 ½ cups cream or use evaporated milk
2 cups flour
5 eggs *(for richer bread, use only yolks)*
1 cup sugar
1 cup melted and slightly cooled butter
1 ½ teaspoons salt
2 teaspoons fresh ground cardamon
1 cup golden raisins
1 cup scalded and cooled milk
2 cups rye flour
2 cups whole wheat flour
2 to 2 ½ cups unbleached flour

Directions

Dissolve yeast in the water in a large bowl. Stir in the cream or evaporated milk and the 2 cups of flour. Beat until smooth. Cover and let rise in a warm place until it has doubled in size. Stir in the eggs, sugar, butter, salt, cardamom, and raisins. Beat until thoroughly combined. Stir in the rye flour and the milk. Add the remaining flour to form a stiff dough. Knead until smooth. Butter or oil a large bowl and place the dough in the bowl. Grease top of dough, cover with a cloth, and let rise until double in size.

Punch dough down and work into a ball. Divide into three equal parts. Place in 3 round cake pans or 3 loaf pans or a combination of these. Let rise until double in size. Bake at 350 degrees until top is golden and a tester comes out clean. Brush top of warm bread with butter or oil. Allow to rest in the pans until partially cool before removing.

If you have cardamon essential oil, you can use it instead of the ground cardamon. It only takes a few drops.

One recipe Gretchen made, which I've made often for company, is spinach timbale. Unlike the instructions in her recipe, I never turn the mold onto a heated platter. I make sure to bake it in a pretty, deep casserole dish and serve it from that.

I have never served this with either the hard boiled eggs or the butter and lemon. There is a handwritten note with the recipe stating that you can use asparagus, chopped cooked brussel sprouts, broccoli, cauliflower, or pureed green peas instead of spinach. I have never used anything but spinach.

a family
Favorite
recipe

Spinach Timbale

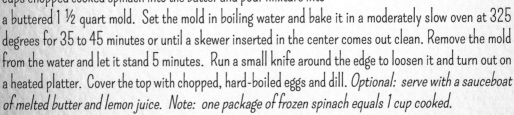

Directions

Cook ½ cup finely chopped onion in 1 tablespoon butter over low heat for 10 minutes without letting them color. Combine the onion with ⅔ cup breadcrumbs, ½ cup grated Gruyere cheese, ½ tsp. salt, and freshly grated nutmeg and cayenne to taste. Beat in 5 eggs, one at a time, and gradually add 1 cup milk, heated ¼ cup butter until the milk is hot and the butter melted. Fold 5 cups chopped cooked spinach into the batter and pour mixture into a buttered 1 ½ quart mold. Set the mold in boiling water and bake it in a moderately slow oven at 325 degrees for 35 to 45 minutes or until a skewer inserted in the center comes out clean. Remove the mold from the water and let it stand 5 minutes. Run a small knife around the edge to loosen it and turn out on a heated platter. Cover the top with chopped, hard-boiled eggs and dill. *Optional: serve with a sauceboat of melted butter and lemon juice. Note: one package of frozen spinach equals 1 cup cooked.*

Memories

Smells trigger intense emotions, bring back memories. Unlike the other senses, the sense of smell goes immediately to the brain because the olfactory bulb is part of the brain's limbic system, an area directly linked to memory and emotion. Months ago, I experienced proof of this when my daughter and I cleaned out her father's apartment in another state. There, on the stairs outside the apartment, I sat down and wrote this poem.

I Watched Movers Box Up a Life

I watched movers box up a life today, a life I thought left me
thirty-some years ago. I was wrong.

When our daughter and I cleaned out the refrigerator, we found
a large pot filled with egusi stew, remnants of the last meal he
cooked. I took the foot-long, hand-carved wooden spoon, scraped dry bits clinging to the sides
of the silver pot. Scrubbing it clean,
smells of memory flooded my nostrils—cayenne, bitter leaves.
It took me ten minutes, ten memory-laden minutes. Even after
scrubbed and dried, the pot's cayenne smell filled my nostrils, the
distinct smell of West African food.

Our daughter and I found papers and photos, items her father
kept all these years, detailed memories of our life together. I
could barely look at them, throat constricting, tears welling
in the eyes of this woman who never cries. Our daughter,
dismayed, told me to go outside. I walked down the quiet
street, brown leaves scattered from autumn, unraked, a strange
street both urban and rural inside a city of nearly half a million
residents. Is this where he walked, attempting to improve his
health? Was I walking in his footsteps?

I watched movers box up a life today, a life I thought left me
thirty-some years ago. I was wrong.

I kept thinking about the first time I saw him, at a party, dazzled by his smile, his dapper clothes, his laugh, totally charmed, later getting married in London, touring Windsor Castle, driving through Cambridge, standing on the white cliffs of Dover, patted down by police because of the IRA when we went shopping at Harrods, and always the endless love letters he wrote me.

Now I recreate versions of Nigerian food, adapting recipes to ingredients I can find locally. Because Amarillo remains one of the largest refugee destinations in the United States, I could find many ingredients there. Various ethnic groups and countries in West Africa have different versions of this. They call it soup, but its consistency is what we would call stew.

West African Soup
(Stew)

Ingredients

1 to 2 pounds meat, *cut into small pieces*

water

1 cup oil

3 tomatoes or use canned tomatoes

1 yellow or white onion, *chopped*

salt and pepper to taste

cayenne—*amount depends on your heat preference—you must use cayenne and make it quite hot or it is not authentic.*

Directions

Stew (boil) the meat in the least amount of water required to make it tender. My husband and I always combined two types of meat, e.g., kidneys and some type of white fish, my favorite combination. If you use fish, do not boil it, add it later. You can use beef or chicken.

Sauté onions in the oil. Add tomatoes, spices and meat and fish, if you use fish, and heat through. You have options to make the stew thicker: add peanut butter or slightly cooked okra. Another option, my preference, is to cook okra on the side and add it to the stew as it is eaten. Some recipes add chopped fresh ginger, garlic, and herbs such as thyme, and even small amounts of curry powder. You do not want to add too much curry; it should not taste like curry because curries come from different cultures.

Serve with rice or foofoo (fufu). With rice, you can eat this with a fork.

If using foofoo, then the only choice is to eat it with your right hand. Traditional foofoo is made from pounded yams and not yams like those here in the US. Others make it with cassava. Foofoo is white and sticky.

Americanized foofoo can be made with instant mashed potatoes and water or mashed potatoes and cream of wheat. Boil water, add the instant mashed potatoes or the mixture, stirring constantly to create a thick ball, thicker than "real" mashed potatoes.

If you want to try to make this foofoo, you can serve it on a big platter where everyone reaches in and gets smaller fingerfuls to dip into the stew, or individuals can put the foofoo and stew on their plates. The mixture of instant mashed potatoes and cream of wheat has a somewhat grainy texture.

Many Somali refugees live in the Amarillo area. The really adventuresome can eat camel meat in at least one restaurant there if ordered in advance. The only East African food I make myself is Ethiopian. Primarily, I use one particular spice: berbere. Be careful when you purchase berbere. Really good berbere is a complex mixture of many spices and not overly hot. Lucky me, I get mine from my friend's mom in Ethiopia. When we visited there, I liked it so much I brought three kilos home. When we run out, we order more

from her. Penzies Spice Company has berbere, but it seems to be mostly cayenne. I have not tried others. Experiment. Maybe try to make your own. One recipe on the Internet combines ginger, chili, paprika, cardamon, coriander, nutmeg, cloves, cinnamon, allspice, and fenugreek.

The berbere I use works well with many kinds of foods, and most people do not find it too hot. I experimented using it with fish and also vegetarian dishes. Here are several recipes in which I have used bebere. I especially make this salmon one when I have company for dinner. It is easy, requires no last-minute work, and everyone who likes salmon enjoys it. Actually, people who think they do not like salmon often find this to their liking as well. If you are unsure, use pink salmon; it is less strongly flavored.

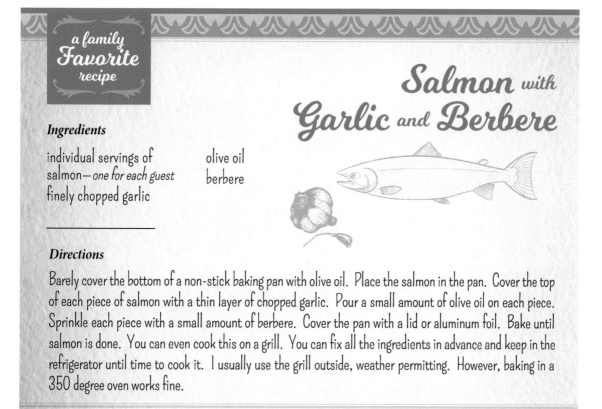

a family
Favorite
recipe

Salmon with Garlic and Berbere

Ingredients

individual servings of salmon—*one for each guest*
finely chopped garlic

olive oil
berbere

Directions

Barely cover the bottom of a non-stick baking pan with olive oil. Place the salmon in the pan. Cover the top of each piece of salmon with a thin layer of chopped garlic. Pour a small amount of olive oil on each piece. Sprinkle each piece with a small amount of berbere. Cover the pan with a lid or aluminum foil. Bake until salmon is done. You can even cook this on a grill. You can fix all the ingredients in advance and keep in the refrigerator until time to cook it. I usually use the grill outside, weather permitting. However, baking in a 350 degree oven works fine.

ETHIOPIA

Ethiopia surprised me. The northwest of the country contains high mountains, many over 13,000 feet, and in summer, daily rain. I kept thinking of photos of Ireland—endless emerald. I have never been so cold and wet as the night we spent in the hotel at Simien Mountains National Park above 12,000 feet. Although perfectly furnished, the rooms lacked heat; at bedtime they gave everyone hot water bottles to put in our beds to warm us up. The next day we hiked through mist and rain. I went with the official guide, and suddenly we became surrounded by gelada, the last of the grass-eating primates.

Later, we visited fairytale-like castles no longer inhabited. Who could resist visiting the Castles of Gondor? I kept thinking of movie sets even when I saw the cages for the lions. Ethiopian lions are different from other African lions, smaller and black-maned. The guide took us to the perfect Ethiopian restaurant where we dined on specialties which, of course, contained berbere.

However, when we drove south and east to Awash National Park, a new Ethiopia appeared, one more like the photos we see in the US, semiarid, herds of big-horned cattle, goats, and camels. Ethiopia exports camels to the Arabian Peninsula for meat.

Ethiopia seemed perfectly safe to me and still does in spite of the following incident. On the drive to Awash National Park, one car tire blew out.

Ethiopia seemed perfectly safe to me and still does in spite of the following incident.

While Dino, my Ethiopian friend, and his dad changed the tire, Dino's wife, his mom, and I stood around watching. First, a man came along and offered to help. His truck had broken down, and he was waiting for help himself—we were on the major highway between Adama, Ethiopia, and Djibouti. Then an Afar teenager walked up and looked around, saying nothing. I realized he had a dagger in the back of his pants when he strolled off. Finally, an Afar man, maybe in his late 40s or 50s, appeared out of the bush. The Afar are nomads who have lived in Ethiopia for thousands of years. The men, noted for their ferocity, lead unchanged lives except now they carry assault rifles slung over their shoulders instead of spears. This man's weapons included both a Kalishnakov and a dagger. Tall, dark, finely featured, he walked around the car, came up to me. Neither of us knowing the other's language, the tiny conversation consisted of gestures. Dino suddenly directed me to get in the car. I ignored him. A couple of minutes passed; Dino loudly repeated the order. I complied, wondering why, a bit miffed. The man eventually wandered off.

When I asked Dino why he instructed me to get in the car, he replied, "You never know what the Afar are going to do. Didn't you notice how close he stood to you?" I never noticed; I have no personal space. Dino feared the man would abduct me. I never felt fear.

I created this recipe about four months after visiting Ethiopia. It works well with cod as well as tilapia. Tilapia is a favored fish in Ethiopia. At Lake Tana, where the Blue Nile begins, we went out in a boat early one morning, and we saw numerous fishermen headed out in the same papyrus boats used thousands of years ago.

This recipe makes good-sized portions for two people.

Tilapia with Beets, Red Peppers, Swiss Chard, and Berbere

Ingredients

2 tilapia filets
½ red onion, *coarsely chopped*
1 red bell pepper, *chopped into bite-sized pieces*
1 medium-sized beet, *thinly sliced*
2 handfuls Swiss chard—*if large pieces, take knife and separate middle spine from the leaf part*
olive oil
bebere

Directions

Chop the spines into ½ inch pieces. Cover the bottom of a large skillet with olive oil. Add the onions, beets, and chopped spines of the Swiss chard. Sauté until the onions are somewhat caramelized and the beets are tender. Add peppers and 1-2 tablespoons of berbere to taste. When the peppers are half done, add the filets. Sprinkle extra berbere over the filets. When they are almost tender, add the Swiss chard and sauté until the Swiss chard wilts. Serve over rice.

PERSIAN FOOD

Because of several years married to an Iranian, I became quite fond of Persian food, especially the way they make rice. It is time consuming in some respects because, although easy, it requires multiple steps. I always use white Basmati rice from either Pakistan or India which I purchase in ten pound bags at either the local Afghani or Syrian market—way cheaper than buying the same rice at the regular grocery store.

My husband used to joke that he knew 101 ways to cook rice. I recall two we made rather often. Basically, they start with the same procedures as the plain rice up to the point when you scoop the partially cooked rice onto the top of the tortilla.

a family
Favorite
recipe

Persian-Style Rice

Ingredients

2 cups rice
4 cups water *or enough to allow the rice to roll around freely in a large pot*

salt to taste
1 large flour tortilla or chapatti
melted butter

Directions

Rinse rice until water runs clear. Add rice to boiling water and boil until the rice grains easily break between thumb and index finger but not done. Rice should still be firm. Drain rice in a colander. Dry bottom of the large pot and cover with a thin layer of melted butter. Place tortilla or chapatti at bottom of pot over the butter. Scoop the rice onto the tortilla one spoonful at a time, making sure it forms a cone. Do not let the rice touch the sides of the pot. With the handle of a wooden spoon, punch several holes through the rice all the way down to the tortilla. Pour melted butter over top of the rice. Place several layers of paper towels or a thick tea towel over the pot. Place lid firmly on top. Cook at medium low heat for 30 to 40 minutes. To test, place small amount of water on index finger and touch side of pot. If it sizzles, the rice is done.

I always use white Basmati rice from either Pakistan or India.

Rice *with* Chicken *and* Saffron

Directions

While rice is boiling, sauté one finely chopped, medium-sized onion in oil or butter. Add one large diced chicken breast to the onion and sauté until tender. Do not overcook the chicken. After rice is drained, add the onion and chicken mixture to the rice. Scoop onto the tortilla exactly as in the instructions for Persian Rice. Mix several strands of saffron with melted butter and pour over the top of the rice cone. Finish as for Persian-style rice.

Rice *with* Beef, Green Beans, *and* Tarragon

Directions

Follow previous instructions with these exceptions: use a tender beef cut, e.g., as in beef for fajitas, and add green beans and tarragon to taste. Omit saffron from the butter in step before final cooking.

What is truly special about these rice dishes is the surprise at the bottom of the pot. After you spoon out all the rice, you discover this delectable, crunchy, golden mixture at the bottom.

Just thinking about it makes me smile, my mouth water. A picture of the reaction I see on friends' faces when they taste it floats through my vision.

OTHER TYPES OF RICE

Rice varies greatly. If I make Asian food, usually Jasmine rice seems appropriate. For a healthier version, as opposed to white Jasmine rice, I use red or black (purple) or mix the two half and half. Both red and black rice contain more nutrients than brown rice which I do not like. In my quest for optimal health, I've tried brown rice repeatedly but can barely eat it, so I gave up. To cook black or red Jasmine rice use the following recipe but know it will take twice the amount of cooking time, e.g., an hour.

Basmati rice works well with several recipes mentioned later in the book, e.g. gallo pinto. It has the lowest glycemic index rating compared to other types of rice. It is longer grained and "drier," less sticky. Both Basmati and Jasmine white rice require about ½ hour cooking time.

Below is my recipe for cooking all types of rice dishes except Persian. This works with white, red, and black rice.

Basmati and other long-grained rice will have more separate grains and be "drier" than red or black rice. Sometimes I combine all three in equal proportions. Red and black rice combined half and half become a beautiful purple color when cooked.

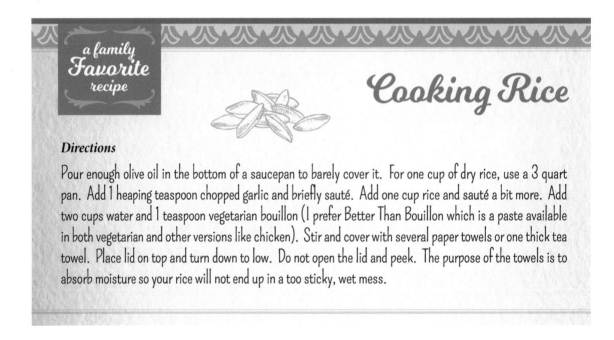

a family **Favorite** *recipe*

Cooking Rice

Directions

Pour enough olive oil in the bottom of a saucepan to barely cover it. For one cup of dry rice, use a 3 quart pan. Add 1 heaping teaspoon chopped garlic and briefly sauté. Add one cup rice and sauté a bit more. Add two cups water and 1 teaspoon vegetarian bouillon (I prefer Better Than Bouillon which is a paste available in both vegetarian and other versions like chicken). Stir and cover with several paper towels or one thick tea towel. Place lid on top and turn down to low. Do not open the lid and peek. The purpose of the towels is to absorb moisture so your rice will not end up in a too sticky, wet mess.

This works with white, red, and black rice.

EATING WITH FRIENDS

Friends come over to my house for food, fun conversation, and to stand on the patio hanging off a cliff. They listen for the hoot owl, watch for deer, sometimes see foxes. When dark comes, they go out to listen to the silence and star gaze.

Many, after repeated visits, make food requests. My friend Anabel from Chihuahua has a husband who says he will only come if I make those black beans and chocolate spiders. Don't become too alarmed, chocolate spiders are no-bake cookies. This black bean casserole is one of my most requested dishes. I never ate black beans until I lived in Veracruz one winter decades ago. No red, white, or pinto beans there, only frijoles negros. Now my preferred beans for this recipe, gallo pinto, chili, and just to eat are frijoles negros, black beans.

When I make this black bean casserole I never measure anything. I cook by feel and taste. Due to requests for the recipe, I finally measured, paid close attention to the process, and wrote down this version.

a family
Favorite
recipe

Refried Black Bean Casserole

Ingredients

2 cans black beans, *drained, or the equivalent if you have cooked dry beans*
enough olive oil to cover the bottom of a large skillet
½ onion, *very finely chopped*
3-4 teaspoons organic ketchup

3 teaspoons ground cumin or to taste. *You may use cumin essential oil—3 to 4 drops.*
tortillas
white cheese, *grated; I usually use Monterey Jack*

Directions

Heat oil in skillet, add onion, and cook until translucent. Place beans in skillet with onions. Take a regular table fork and mash the beans repeatedly until most of the beans are mashed—I like to leave a few unmashed ones to add to the texture. This is easier if you do one can at a time. Thoroughly mix onions and beans. Add cumin and ketchup; keep mixing until the mixture is thick and heated through. Using a round slow cooker or casserole dish, oil the bottom of the dish, place one tortilla in the bottom. Place enough black beans on the tortilla to cover it thoroughly. Sprinkle grated cheese on top. Repeat these layers until you have used up all the black bean mixture. End with grated cheese on top. Heat through until cheese is melted.

I use an old, round slow cooker for this recipe. However, a round casserole will work. You can use any kind of tortillas. Some, usually flour, are almost the right size to fit perfectly in a round slow cooker. However, corn tortillas are healthier because of no sodium. They also allow gluten-free guests to eat this dish.

You may make the bean mixture a day in advance and store in the refrigerator. If you do this, allow more time for heating the mixture and melting the cheese.

Serving suggestions: I usually serve this with rice, salad, and some meat or other dish. Many of my friends are vegetarians and this offers an easy make-ahead dish. You can increase the amounts to serve quite a few guests. This casserole also goes well with platanos fritos, fried plantains.

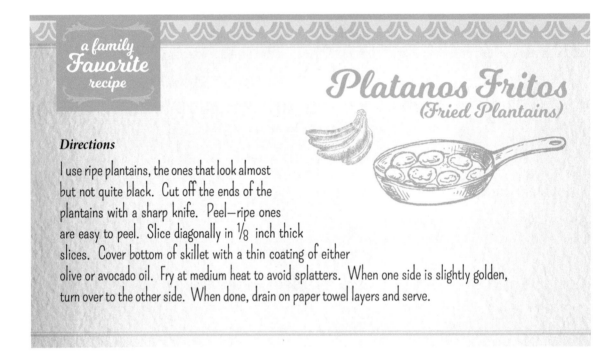

a family **Favorite** *recipe*

Platanos Fritos
(Fried Plantains)

Directions

I use ripe plantains, the ones that look almost but not quite black. Cut off the ends of the plantains with a sharp knife. Peel—ripe ones are easy to peel. Slice diagonally in $\frac{1}{8}$ inch thick slices. Cover bottom of skillet with a thin coating of either olive or avocado oil. Fry at medium heat to avoid splatters. When one side is slightly golden, turn over to the other side. When done, drain on paper towel layers and serve.

Some people prefer green plantains. They have to be peeled with a knife. The end result is starchier and less sweet.

Chocolate Spiders

Ingredients

2 Hersey dark chocolate bars
for a total of 8-9 ounces
of dark chocolate

2 cups crisp rice, *e.g,*
Rice Krispies
½ cup shredded coconut

Directions

Melt chocolate in a large saucepan on very low heat. Remove from heat and add crisp rice and coconut. Thoroughly mix. Drop from a teaspoon onto a lightly greased cookie sheet or a large piece of wax paper. Refrigerate until set. I use a cookie sheet and put it in the freezer. After they are set, you can put them in a bowl and keep in the refrigerator. If you do not like coconut, you can use more crisp rice or add some finely chopped pecans or walnuts. Black walnuts are especially good with the chocolate.

Chocolate Spiders make a particularly good dessert for summer because you do not have to heat up the oven. You can serve them alone or with ice cream for the perfect summer dessert.

GO-TO PROTEIN

Although I am not a vegetarian, I rarely eat red meat and chicken only occasionally. My go-to protein source is fish, especially salmon and cod. In addition to the salmon with berbere recipe earlier in the book, I have two other favorite salmon recipes. All salmon recipes can be made with pink salmon for a less fishy eating experience and work well with guests who are not necessarily lovers of salmon. The first time I ate Teriyaki Salmon was at my son's house years ago. I usually cook it on the grill, but it can be baked in the oven or even sautéed on the stovetop if you are in a hurry or cooking only for one or two.

a family
Favorite
recipe

Teriyaki Salmon *with* Crystallized Ginger

Ingredients

salmon—*one serving-sized piece for each person*
teriyaki sauce to cover salmon for marinade—*I use reduced sodium*

crystallized ginger, *coarsely chopped*
chopped onion or garlic *(optional)*
olive oil

Directions

Cut the salmon into serving-sized pieces. Arrange in a baking dish or pan so that you can pour an equal amount of teriyaki sauce over each piece. Marinate for several hours or overnight. The intensity of the fish taste will depend on the length of time the fish is in the marinade. If you are using the onion or garlic, sauté it in olive oil until done. Pour evenly over the pieces of fish. Finally, place equal amounts of the crystallized ginger over each piece. Cover the baking pan or dish with either a lid or aluminum foil. If using a grill, heat grill to 350, place pan on grill, and grill until salmon is done. If the pan is not non-stick, you may wish to remove the marinade and salmon from the pan, wipe it clean, and place olive oil in the bottom before returning the salmon and marinade to the pan and proceeding with the process. Follow same directions for using an oven. If cooking on your stovetop, separately marinate the salmon, sauté the onions or garlic in the pan and then add the salmon and marinade. Cook until salmon is tender.

Crystallized ginger is sweet with a bit of heat.
Use the amount that suits your taste.

Serve over Jasmine rice with a fresh salad made with greens, red bell peppers, carrot circles, scallions cut into circles, and finely chopped red cabbage.

Every time I make this sort of salad, I think of one of my exchange students,

Gaston Luis Zulaica del Sueldo. He told me he always made salads for his grandmother; every night when we had salad, he fixed it. I wrote a prose poem about him. The following is an excerpt from that poem.

Every night while I fix dinner, he sits at the brown Knabe piano my parents gave me thirty years ago and plays and plays: Beethoven, the theme from Twilight, Chopin...I look up from chopping onions and see the short, dark ringlets on the back of his neck and watch his gliding, long fingered hands. He plays until salad making time arrives. He tells me he makes salads for his grandmother back home. Now he makes them for us: layers of emerald lettuce, red peppers, black olives, orange carrots, green onions, a kaleidoscope of appetizing color.

Another favorite salmon recipe involves a very unusual combination of ingredients: rosemary and grapes. Salmon remains one of the easiest dishes to make for company. These two recipes, along with the one containing berbere, allow me to cook three totally different, easy recipes for company, all containing healthy salmon.

Salmon with Rosemary and Grapes

Ingredients

one portion salmon for each person
poblano peppers, *coarsely chopped, allow ¼ cup per person*
red grapes—*five cut in half for each portion*
finely chopped sprigs of rosemary or use rosemary essential oil
one medium sized clove garlic per person, *finely chopped*
olive oil

Directions

In a non-stick skillet, cover bottom with olive oil and sauté the garlic and chopped rosemary sprigs. If using rosemary essential oil, take care to use sparingly. A little goes a long way. When both are slightly browned, add the salmon. When the salmon is half done, add poblano peppers. Sauté until salmon is done and the peppers are cooked but still bright green. Finally, add the grapes and cook just long enough to heat through. Serve with rice. For this recipe I usually use Basmati rice, not Jasmine.

I have a friend who is very allergic to garlic. For all the recipes using garlic, whenever this friend is a guest, I use onions instead of garlic.

Although I cook salmon often, usually a couple times per week, one of my favorite fish recipes features cod loins. It is quick and easy and something I can cook after a long day at work without a lot of time and effort. This is important because I teach English Language Arts, and frequently a stack of papers need grading after work. I make this recipe for two people even though I live alone. It is delicious left over, and then I have another meal ready to reheat in the microwave. When I make pasta or rice, I make extra for the same reason. While some foods may not warm up well, rice and pasta taste nearly the same as freshly cooked.

a family
Favorite
recipe

Cod Loin with Fennel and Lemon

Ingredients

2 small cod loins *or one large cut in half*
3 cloves garlic, *chopped*
1 poblano pepper, *seeded and coarsely chopped*
fennel essential oil
lemon essential oil
vegetables of your choice, *cut into bite-sized pieces*
handful unsalted pepitas
olive oil

Directions

Vary this by using different vegetables, e.g., spinach, Swiss chard, Brussels sprouts, beets, carrots.

Sauté the garlic in olive oil until barely golden. If you use beets or carrots, sauté them with the garlic until nearly tender. If you use spinach, beet greens, Swiss chard, add them last.

Add the cod loins to the garlic mixture and sprinkle each one with several drops of lemon and fennel essential oil. If you do not use essential oil, sprinkle with ground fennel and add seeded sliced lemons. If using Brussels sprouts, cut them in slices and add at the same time as the cod. When the cod is half cooked, add the poblano peppers and cook only until cod is done and the peppers are cooked but still bright green. If using spinach, or Swiss chard, add just before cod and peppers are done and stir until wilted. Add pepitas. Serve over pasta or rice.

I have also used fresh fennel for this recipe.
Sauté it along with the garlic.

Vegetarian

For company, especially groups larger than four or five, I use several "go to" recipes: one of the salmon dishes, rice, roasted vegetables, salad. For vegetarian company sometimes I add soyrizo (chorizo made with soy rather than pork) to the roasted vegetables. If you use soyrizo, you will need to take it out of the casing and break it up into bite-sized pieces.

This is another of those dishes you can prepare in advance before company arrives. Simply place on the grill, timed for when you want to serve dinner. This usually requires 30 to 45 minutes, depending on the amount of vegetables and type of pan. To up the protein count and remain vegetarian, add a can of drained garbanzo beans toward the end so they can heat through before serving.

a family Favorite recipe

Roasted Vegetables

Ingredients

heavy skillet, casserole, or baking dish
purple potatoes
poblano peppers, *seeded*
carrots
red bell peppers, *seeded*
beets

Brussels sprouts
jalapeño peppers, seeded *(optional)*
avocado oil *(or use olive)*
spices—*mixed Italian, berbere, cumin, coriander, your pick*

Directions

Cut the vegetables into large bite-sized pieces. Do not bother to peel. It is a waste of time; the peel adds nutrients. Use an appropriate amount of vegetables for the number of guests. Pour avocado oil to cover bottom of your cooking utensil. Layer vegetables, adding small amounts of oil and spices as you go. When all the vegetables are in the pan, place pan on a grill heated to 400 degrees. You can also place on a cold grill and allow them to heat as the grill heats. Roast until vegetables are done and slightly browned. Check and stir often to avoid sticking. Add more oil if necessary. Do NOT overcook. You can also bake this in the oven at 400-425 degrees.

Note: If you have low thyroid, eat cooked vegetables rather than raw vegetables. Many vegetables we frequently eat raw depress thyroid function. This list includes kale and broccoli because they contain high amounts of goitrogen. Also, when cooking at high temperatures, avocado oil may be a better choice. Olive oil has a lower smoke point than avocado oil, and this smoke point varies depending on the type of olive oil. Extra virgin olive oil has a smoke point below 400.

Because several of my friends are vegetarian, I invented recipes that do not taste particularly vegetarian so that I can serve them to all guests present without having to create separate meat dishes. Even non-vegetarians request this recipe.

a family
Favorite
recipe

Vegetarian Enchiladas

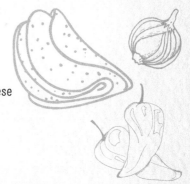

Ingredients

six tortillas *(for this dish I use flour, but corn are healthier because of sodium)*
½ purple onion, *finely chopped*
1 large poblano pepper, *finely chopped*
½ medium-sized red bell pepper, *finely chopped*
1 8-ounce package cream cheese
olive oil

1 teaspoon Mexican spice mix
½ teaspoon ground chipotle pepper *(I use Spice Appeal— adjust for hotness or omit)*
shredded Monterey Jack cheese
red enchilada sauce—*you can make your own or use canned*

Directions

Sauté onions and peppers in just enough olive oil so they will not stick or become too dry. Mix in cream cheese and spices until thoroughly blended. Fill the tortillas, roll up, and place in an 8-inch casserole dish. Cover with a light layer of the enchilada sauce. Sprinkle enough shredded cheese on top to cover the enchiladas. Cover with aluminum foil. Bake in a 350 degree oven for 30-40 minutes.

The following sauce also works for vegetarian friends and can be used for enchiladas or tamales. My Mexican opera singer friend, Jesus, told me this is the best tamale sauce he had ever tasted.

Garlic Cream Sauce

Pour enough olive oil into a medium-sized saucepan to cover the bottom about ¼ inch deep. Coarsely chop ½ medium sized onion and two cloves garlic. Sauté in the olive oil. When the onion appears translucent, pour the onion mixture and 1 ½ cups half and half into a blender. Add two tablespoons flour and ½ teaspoon ground chipotle chili powder. Blend until onions and garlic are pureed. Return mixture to the saucepan and cook over low heat until thickened. Pour over tamales or enchiladas and warm thoroughly in a 350 degree oven. To increase or decrease the amount of spiciness and "heat," increase or decrease the amount of chipotle powder.

Vegetables are my favorite food. I experiment and create unique recipes using them. Sometimes it works fantastically and sometimes, well, not so much. Recently, after a dinner party, I had leftover vegetables that needed cooking, so I created this recipe.

a family *Favorite* recipe

Vegetables *with* Coriander, Cumin, *and* Tumeric

Ingredients

1 medium-sized beet, *cut into half coins*
1 poblano pepper, *seeded and chopped*
½ onion, *chopped*
several pieces of Swiss chard, *stems removed and chopped, leaves cut into large, bite sized pieces*
several garlic cloves, *peeled and chopped*
olive oil
1 teaspoon coriander seeds, *ground*
½ teaspoon cumin—*or extra to taste*
1 teaspoon ground turmeric

Directions

Sauté the beets, chopped Swiss chard stems, garlic, and onion in olive oil until beets are cooked through. Add spices and poblano pepper. When pepper is nearly done, add the Swiss chard leaves and cook only until wilted.

Serve over rice. Sometimes I combine ⅓ cup each, white, black, and red rice, using the recipe earlier in this book. Be sure not to peek unless you want mushy rice.

Frequently, I blog about food, tell vignettes about my food life, share the events of the day that led up to my cooking a specific recipe.

See my website—*www.julianalightle.com.*
Such is the case with the following blog post.

LAZY DAY AND DINNER

Cool and cloudy reigned today. Now, tornado warnings west of here glide across the TV screen I've turned on mute. About now, the severe thunderstorms are supposed to start. Earlier, I took some photos from my patio after I fed Rosie (my horse) to beat the predicted storm, swept the dirt and little rocks from yesterday's storm off the drive, and strolled around to get some exercise. After several hectic days of no cooking, I decided to cook something vegetarian.

a family Favorite recipe

Brussels Sprouts with Spices

Ingredients

1 medium-sized onion, *coarsely chopped*
6 medium Brussels sprouts, *cut in half*
½ large red bell pepper *coarsely chopped*
1 teaspoon chana masala *(East Indian spice)*
1 teaspoon berbere
olive oil

Directions

Pour enough olive oil in 8-10 inch skillet to cover the bottom. Sauté the onions in the oil until translucent. Add the Brussel sprouts and spices. Stir and cook until the Brussel sprouts are cooked but still crisp. Add the red pepper and sauté. Do not overcook. Serve over Jasmine rice.

ITALIAN

*I created this recipe after buying something
I had never tried before, Tuscan kale.*

a family
Favorite
recipe

Pasta *with* Kale *and* Portabella Mushrooms

Ingredients

extra virgin olive oil
½ medium onion, *coarsely chopped*
3-4 medium-sized portabella mushrooms, *sliced*

3 large Tuscan kale leaves, *center stem removed and then chopped*
Greek oregano
ricotta cheese

Directions

Cover bottom of a skillet with the olive oil. Add onions, mushrooms, and chopped kale stems. Sauté until the onions are translucent and the kale stems cooked, but still crunchy. While this is cooking, tear the kale leaves into bite-sized pieces. Take two dried oregano stems and lightly remove and crumble the leaves and florets into the skillet. Discard the stems. Add the kale leaves to the onion mixture and sauté. When done, kale leaves will be tender but still bright green. Serve over cooked pasta of your choice and place a dollop of ricotta cheese on top.

Greek oregano is very mild. You might want to use less of other types of oregano. Without ricotta, this recipe is vegan. I use whole milk ricotta; I rarely buy low-fat anything. I am pasta picky and prefer Montebello brand from a monastery in Italy established in 1388. My favorite shape is conchiglie.

Sometimes I grow my own Greek oregano and dry a bunch on my countertop. This works because I live in a dry climate. I take two stems with the dried leaves and flowers still attached, strip off the leaves and flowers and crush them with my hands directly into the skillet.

COSTA RICA

When I look at photos of this last Costa Rican trip, it seems hard to believe it was the dry season. We saw large irrigation ditches bringing water all the way from Arenal, a huge lake next to an active volcano on the other side of the mountains. The Nicoya Peninsula there remains one of the Blue Zones, one of those places where a substantial number of people live past 100 years of age. I love their national dish, gallo pinto. The people on the Nicoya Peninsula eat this every day.

This is a dish most people like and a good one if vegetarians are coming for dinner. It is a pretty and colorful dish you can make ahead and re-heat. It is actually better this way because it allows the flavors to meld. It goes well with platanos fritos and the cabbage salad recipe on page 61.

a family
Favorite
recipe

Gallo Pinto

Ingredients

enough vegetable oil to lightly cover bottom of a skillet
1 ½ cups day-old cooked rice
1 cup cooked black beans
1 medium onion, *finely diced*
1 small, sweet red bell pepper, *finely diced*
2 tablespoons chopped cilantro *(optional)*
1 teaspoon ground cumin *(optional)*

Directions

Sauté onions until tender. Add peppers and sauté. Then add beans. Finally, add the rice and heat through, stirring constantly. There should be just enough juice from the beans to color the rice but not too much. I usually use garlic instead of onion, and poblano peppers instead of the red or use a combination of both. When cooking this for myself rather than for company, I use equal amounts of beans and rice because I want the extra protein from the beans. My preference is to add the cumin but not the cilantro. Experiment to see what suits you.

For a more colorful dish, combine seeded, chopped poblano peppers with the red.

In tropical, lower altitudes, lettuce does not grow well. Salad consists of various versions using cabbage, somewhat like coleslaw in the US but without the creamy dressing. I could never quite duplicate the salads of this sort in Costa Rica; however, this comes close.

a family
Favorite
recipe

Colorful Cabbage Salad

Ingredients

1 medium head purple cabbage, *finely chopped*
1 cup thinly sliced baby carrots
1 cup finely chopped broccoli
1 handful of rings from leek stalk *(optional)*
equal amounts of olive oil, sweet chili sauce, and mirin
(Japanese sweet cooking rice wine) to make ⅓ to ½ cup
measure when combined

Directions

Mix all the above ingredients and chill. If allergic to garlic, I omit the sweet chili sauce. It has garlic in it.

This bright salad not only looks lovely, it also packs a lot of nutrition, is easy, and can be made in advance.

Several years ago I took my first trip to Costa Rica with my friend, a high school Spanish teacher from Mexico whose husband adores the black bean casserole discussed earlier in this book. I also teach, and we took some of our students with us. A few years later, I returned with my daughter, Ema, and grandson.

Costa Rica remains an easy place to safely eat the food, drink the water, and experience adventures from the simple to the daunting—your pick. The first time I went in the summer and the last time with Ema and grandson during Christmas holidays. To save money, choose summer—way cheaper. Although both times involved tours, the final adventure occurred when we rented a car; Ema drove. Compared to many other countries, driving there seems easy. For the most part, people follow the rules, do not careen at high speeds down the road, and usually drive in a manner that we, in the U.S., would consider normal driving.

Because Christmas vacation is prime tourist season, I reserved a hotel on the Pacific side down near the Nicoya Peninsula in early September. A month before departure, I received an email informing me that they had screwed up and we had no hotel room at the place I had reserved. Panicked, I searched and searched and searched. Nothing unless I wanted to pay more than 500 dollars a night. Finally, after hours on the Internet, I located a place near Playa Negra, farther down on the Nicoya Peninsula. The photos looked lovely, and I guessed its better price correlated to its cash only requirement. We arrived. Although rather Spartan and elementary, it seemed ok. We unpacked, headed out to eat dinner in the nearby town, bought some groceries. The waiter's reaction when he asked where we were staying should have been a forewarning; we missed it.

After eating some of the best pizza ever, we returned to the room. Ants, biting ants, had invaded; someone had turned the air conditioner off. We tried to discuss the circumstances with the French owner who refused to talk to me in Spanish (his English lacked). None of my family speak French. After he screamed at Ema, we convinced him, with his wife's help, to return my cash, packed up, and left.

I guessed we would spend the night in the vehicle—a large SUV Ema had convinced the rental guy to provide us for the same price as the tiny one. Where would we find a place to even park for the night? After we arrived at the main road, Ema, undaunted, recalled seeing the entrance to another hotel down the road. She drove down its drive, stopped at the office at ten at night. I walked into the office. No one was there. Ema rolled down her window and called to me, "Mom, a guy is walking up the road. Go talk to him." I did, explaining in Spanish—he did not speak English—that we needed a room for three nights. He looked at the registry; someone had left in an emergency. They had a room for two nights. He led us there. His key did not work; later I learned that he was the security guard. He called the manager who let us in, told us we could pay in the morning, when he also wanted me to tell him why we were out wandering around in the middle of the night.

Talk about luck!! The room astonished us, an entire, huge cabana to ourselves. When I walked out the next morning in search of coffee, the view nearly bowled me over.

This remains one of my favorite Costa Rican memories: superb café con leche; open air restaurant overlooking a pristine beach; families with children and young men playing soccer; an excellent dinner with various meats roasted over a roaring fire; horseback riding through a jungle, a little village, dunes above the beach, then galloping back along the water.

STUFFED ACORN SQUASH

Winter squash, butternut and acorn, are two vegetables I like and think are underused. Because I became tired of peeling butternut, I decided to invent something for acorn squash. Much to my surprise this was one of Martina's favorite foods. Martina, an exchange student from Milano, Italy, lived with me for one semester while attending high school. She even sent photos home to her mother to see if the squash was sold there so her family could try it.

The following recipe is for two. Obviously, just buy more squash and increase the other ingredients if you want to make it for more people. This is a perfect recipe for vegetarians and vegans because it contains no meat, fish, or dairy.

1 acorn squash, cut in half, seeds removed

½ medium sized onion, finely chopped

½ to 1 tsp honey for each half

Pepitas or any chopped nuts of your choice

Sauté the finely chopped onion in olive oil until translucent. Stir in one handful of seeds or nuts. Rub olive oil in the bottom of a small baking dish or pan and cover the flesh of the squash with a thin layer of olive oil. Place squash in the pan, fill center with the onion mixture. Place honey on top of this mixture. Bake in a 400 degree oven for 30-45 minutes, depending on the size of the squash halves.

Serve with salad.

BRISKET

This recipe originated as an unplanned blog post after entertaining ten guests on a hot summer day. The compliments encouraged me to remember how I made it and write it down. The only time I ever make brisket occurs when I expect quite a few guests and I do not want much to do just before I serve the food. There is another reason I like to cook brisket in the summer. I can use my electric roaster and plug it into the outlet on the patio and not heat up the house. Since I do not particularly like barbeque, I do something different, a sort of Tex-Mex recipe.

Brisket for a Crowd

Ingredients

1 4 to 5-pound brisket, *trimmed of fat*

1 large onion, *coarsely chopped*

cumin, *enough to completely cover the top of the brisket when sprinkled on it*

2-3 tablespoons Mexican chili seasoning

1-2 teaspoons coriander, *ground (optional)*

brown sugar

1 bottle cheap, dry red wine

1 15-ounce can chopped, salt free tomatoes

4-5 jalapeño peppers *(optional)*

Directions

Place brisket in a roaster, fat side down and pour in the red wine to a depth of 1½ inches. Cover the top with the cumin and chili seasoning. Evenly scatter the chopped onions over the top. Bake at 325 for two hours. Turn the brisket over so that the fat side is up. Bake another 1-2 hours. Turn the temperature down to 275 and turn over again so the fat side is down. Cover the top of the brisket with the tomatoes. Sprinkle two small handfuls of brown sugar over the top of the tomatoes. If using coriander, sprinkle it over the brown sugar. Check to make sure the broth is not becoming too dry and add extra wine if necessary. Bake another 1-2 hours. If using jalapeños, cut into halves and seed. Add them about one hour before serving. Usually, I cook brisket 6-7 hours. I do not want it to become too dry, but I do want the juices to cook down so that they create a natural sauce for the meat without adding any thickening. Just before serving, slice the brisket into pieces and stir around so the sauce covers all the pieces of meat. I like to use jalapeños this way because it does not increase the "heat" for those who do not like hot food, but there are tasty tidbits of hot for those who do.

For a smaller group of people, use a chuck roast and adjust the amount of other ingredients to the size of the roast. If a small size, I cook it in a crockpot.

DESSERT

Except for Mom's recipes and the Chocolate Spiders, I rarely make dessert. When I invite guests, I feel lucky. Several friends love dessert making. One from Peru brings flan, another from Indonesia sometimes brings mango pudding, and another bakes crème brulee of all flavors, including lavender and lemon verbena. Why should I even bother making dessert with friends like this?

One year when I grew more zucchini than I knew what to do with, I invented this recipe. It is healthy—well, as healthy as cake can be—easy, moist, keeps well, and freezable with no ill effects. Since it contains chocolate, most love it.

a family **Favorite** *recipe*

Chocolate Zucchini Cake

Directions

Combine 3 eggs, 1 ⅔ cups sugar, and 1 cup cooking oil (I use light olive oil) in an electric mixer bowl. Add 1 teaspoon vanilla. Mix thoroughly. Combine 1 ½ cups flour, 1 teaspoon ground cinnamon, ¼ teaspoon baking powder, 1 teaspoon baking soda, and ¼ cup dark cocoa. Stir thoroughly. Sift. Add to egg mixture and mix in mixing bowl. By hand mix in 2 cups grated zucchini and ¾ cups chopped walnuts. The mixture will be stiff. Spoon into an oiled and floured Bundt pan. Bake at 325-350 degrees for 1 hour or until done. Do not over bake. Let cool before taking out of bundt pan. Turn onto large plate or platter. Sift confectioners sugar over the top *(optional)*.

When sifting dry ingredients, sift onto waxed paper for easy clean-up.

FINAL THOUGHTS ON FOOD AND LIFE

By now everyone knows that to a large extent you are what you eat. For some that translates into a strict regimen only few can follow. Lucky me, my favorite foods remain mostly vegetables, and I snack on nuts, usually almonds and pistachios. When a child, I helped Mom grow peas, broccoli, tomatoes, green beans, parsnips, turnips, beets, lettuce, radishes, cabbage; you name it, we grew it. Only a few currently popular vegetables escaped Mom's gardening list, Swiss chard, kale, spinach. Personally, I prefer Swiss chard and spinach to kale. We ate greens, especially in the spring, wild greens we collected. I regret no longer remembering what exactly we collected. Dandelions. Yes. What else? Purslane maybe. I do not know. Except for the dandelions, I doubt I could identify them. Every spring I walk around looking, thinking but really do not know what to pick. This makes me sad.

As humans, we often associate food with family, friends, happiness. Food is life. As for happiness, I agree with Abraham Lincoln that people are about as happy as they decide to be. Good health, fine friends and family help.

Healthy eating requires some effort I admit. Most restaurant and prepackaged food contain too much sodium and sugar. Often healthier food choices cost more. However, this becomes less true as more of us choose healthy food options. Here the law of supply and demand holds true. The more we buy healthier options, the cheaper they become.

Soil matters. Healthier soil creates plants that contain more vitamins and minerals. When followed, current agricultural science enables farmers to make better choices without sacrificing profit.

Several years ago, on the advice of a pharmacist friend, I decided to investigate Blood-Type-related food choices. As a consequence, I experimented with the Type A recommended diet and found that my digestive system works better when I use many of the recommended food choices. By experimenting, I found I could add some foods not on the diet, e.g., some hard cheeses, garbanzo beans, poblano peppers. I avoid foods in the nightshade family such as potatoes, peppers, and tomatoes. You will find few tomatoes and potatoes in the recipes in this book. Experimenting to see what works for you remains very important. Feeling well pays off.

Bon appetit!

ACKNOWLEDGMENTS

The possibility of this book arises from a lifetime of cooking with and for friends and family. I want to especially thank my son Erik Karlsson and my daughter Ema Mowoe for eating my food experiments since childhood. In addition, I want to thank my grandson D'mitri Herrero for helping me cook and Ema for insisting I forge ahead and do this.

Thanks to Katelynn Butler and Nathalie Cantly for original read throughs and suggestions and, more recently, Katelynn for proofing. Thanks to Jennifer Archer for her editing services. Thanks to Lucy Jimenez and Mitch Khoury at Cramer Marketing for taking this to publication ready.

Ema collects cookbooks. Her critiques of photos and layout proved extremely helpful. She repeatedly and patiently took endless photos for the book and critiqued mine.

Thanks to my friends and family who exposed me to foods worldwide from Sweden to Iran to Africa to Latin America and beyond.

Index *of* Recipes

BREAD

Mom's Bran Muffins	11
Mom's Pumpkin Bread	10
Rye Bread with Cardamon	27

DESSERTS

Chocolate Spiders	41
Chocolate Zucchini Cake	69
Grandma's Strawberry Shortcake	21
Mom's Pie Crust	13
Mom's Pumpkin Pie	14
One Egg Cake and Topping	16

CHICKEN

Rice with Chicken and Saffron	37

FISH

Cod Loin with Fennel and Lemon	47
Mom's Salmon Loaf	07
Salmon with Garlic and Berbere	31
Salmon with Rosemary and Grapes	45
Tilapia with Beets, Red Pepper, Swiss Chard, and Berbere	35
Teriyaki Salmon with Crystallized Ginger	42

MEAT

Brisket for a Crowd	67
Mom's Hamburger with Tomatoes	09
Mom's Pork Chops	06
Rice with Beef, Green Beans, and Tarragon	37
West African Soup (Stew)	30

SAUCES

Dad's Wine Sauce	22
Garlic Cream Sauce	51

VEGETARIAN

Brussels Sprouts with Spices	55
Celery and Potato Soup	23
Cooking Rice	38
Colorful Cabbage Salad	61
Gallo Pinto	59
Grandma's Noodles	19
Pasta with Kale and Portabella Mushrooms	57
Persian-Style Rice	36
Platanos Fritos	40
Refried Black Bean Casserole	39
Roasted Vegetables	49
Spinach Timbale	28
Stuffed Acorn Squash	66
Sweet Sautéed Apples	11
Vegetarian Enchiladas	51
Vegetables with Coriander, Cumin, and Tumeric	53